McLAREN CARS
1965 - 1996
Photo Album

Text and Photographs by
Norman Hayes

Iconografix
Photo Album Series

Iconografix continuously seeks collections of archival photographs for reproduction in future books. We require a minimum of 120 photographs per subject. We prefer subjects narrow in focus, i.e., a specific model, railroad, racing venue, etc. Photographs must be of high-quality, suited to reproduction in an 8x10-inch format. We willingly pay for the use of photographs.

If you own or know of such a collection, please contact: The Publisher, Iconografix, PO Box 446, Hudson, Wisconsin 54016.

Iconografix
PO Box 446
Hudson, Wisconsin 54016 USA

Text Copyright © 1997

Iconografix books are offered at a discount when sold in quantity for promotional use. Businesses or organizations seeking details should write to the Marketing Department, Iconografix, at the above address.

Library of Congress Card Number 97-70618

ISBN 1-882256-74-3

97 98 99 00 01 02 03 5 4 3 2 1

Printed in the United States of America

Bruce McLaren (center) in the paddock at the Aintree Grand Prix circuit for the 1964 International 200. The Cooper Climax he drove was retired on the sixth lap with an overheating problem. McLaren built his first car in 1964. Following the 1965 season, he left the Cooper Formula 1 team to build his own cars in this category.

INTRODUCTION

Bruce McLaren was born August 30, 1937 in Auckland, on the North Island of New Zealand. His father ran a garage, and often competed in local motorcycle races with some success. His father later gave up the two wheels for four, and started racing cars. So, it was no wonder that the young McLaren took to motor racing with great enthusiasm. At the tender age of 15, just after passing his driving test, Bruce entered his first race.

During his early years, McLaren raced an Ulster Austin Seven, an Austin Healey, an ex-Jack Brabham Cooper sports car, and a Maserati 8CLT, a car originally built for Indianapolis racing just before World War II. Eventually, he drove a Formula 2 car with a Coventry Climax FPF engine bored out to 1750 cc. Racing the single-seater Cooper during 1957 and 1958 with great success, McLaren earned a "Driver to Europe" scholarship that took him to England for a European season of racing. During the European season of 1958 McLaren drove very well, putting a lot of the established drivers in the shade with his superior driving. He was given a works drive by John Cooper for 1959, and won his first World Championship race in the inaugural United States Grand Prix. Afterwards, his career was never in doubt, and he had many successes with the Cooper works team.

The first McLaren car was built in 1964. Developed from the Cooper-Zerex Special raced in the States by Roger Penske, it was originally fitted with a Coventry Climax engine. McLaren fitted it with a 4500 cc Oldsmobile engine, and he went on to win sports car races at Mosport (Canada) and Brands Hatch (England). This led to McLaren's original Group 7 sports car, the McLaren-Elva MK 1A, fitted with an Oldsmobile engine. During 1965, the car had numerous successes in both McLaren's hands and those of some privateers.

Following the 1965 season, Bruce left the Cooper F1 team, and went on to build his own cars in this category. The first car was the McLaren M2B, raced at Monaco with an ex-Indy Ford 4200 cc V-8 reduced in bore and stroke to 3000 cc. It was a heavy engine that did not produce sufficient power to counteract its extra weight. In the next race, the British Grand Prix at Brands Hatch, McLaren changed to the Serenissima or ATS engine. He finished sixth, two laps down.

In 1967 a new car, the M4B, was produced. It used only a 2200 cc BRM engine in the 3000 cc category. Later in the year, the M5A was built with a 3000 cc BRM V-12. The season was a disaster, as far as the results were concerned, with only a fourth and a seventh place to show for all the hard work. It was quite a different story in Group 7 racing. Bruce McLaren became Can-Am champion in a McLaren M6A with Chevrolet V-8, and teammate Denny Hulme took second place in the championship.

The first victory for a McLaren F1 car came in the 1968 Race of Champions at Brands Hatch, with McLaren taking the honors in the new "bathtub" aluminum monocoque M7A Ford Cosworth DFV V-8 car. Later in the year, McLaren won his first F1 Grand Prix, the Belgian at Spa-Francorchamps.

In 1969, British F1 constructors tried to gain an advantage over each other, experimenting with different forms of racing cars. McLaren and several others tried their hands at building four-wheel-drive cars. The McLaren M9A Ford DFV V-8 4WD car was debuted at the 1969 British Grand Prix at Silverstone, and Derek Bell was secured on loan from Ferrari to drive the car. The car was not very competitive. Bell spun the car, due to a deflating tire, and soon afterwards retired when a rear suspension part broke. The car was never raced again, having been deemed a complete waste of time and money. The year also saw the start of Formula 5000 racing in Great Britain, and Peter Gethin won the opening race at Oulton Park in fine style. He went on to win the British Guards Championship for 1969 in a McLaren M10A powered by a 5.0-liter Chevrolet V-8.

June 2, 1970 will always stand out as a sad day in McLaren Car's history. Bruce McLaren was at the Goodwood racing circuit, which had been closed to racing for more than four years but was still used to test cars, checking out the new M8D Can-Am car. McLaren was driving down a long straight when the massive tail section was ripped away. He lost control of the car and ran broadside into a concrete reinforced earth bank. McLaren's injuries were fatal. Following his death, Teddy Mayer took over the running of the team. The team lacked major results in Grand Prix racing for almost four years, until Emerson Fittipaldi was signed to drive the 3.0-liter M23 Ford DFV V-8 in 1974. Fittipaldi immediately restored the team's confidence by winning the F1 Drivers World Championship, while the team won the F1 Team Constructors Championship.

The 1976 season was a great one for British driver James Hunt, who was signed to drive for the McLaren team. The M23-type car he ran was by then a three-year-old design. Nonetheless, Hunt recorded six wins during the season and, by finishing third overall in the last race of the season in Japan, secured the F1 Drivers World Championship from Niki Lauda by one point.

The team seemed to go into a decline again until the early 1980s, when Marlboro, the team's main sponsor, suggested that McLaren and Ron Dennis' Project Four team merge. The new team, McLaren International, was born in September 1980. John Barnard, a director of McLaren International, designed and had built in the USA the first carbon fiber monocoque. The MP4 (Marlboro-Project 4) monocoque chassis started a revolution in F1 cars, with many other teams later copying the design. The MP4 made its debut in 1981 at the Argentine Grand Prix, with John Watson driving. The car still used the Ford DFV V-8 engine. The car was retired during the race, after a promising start, with severe rear end vibration.

Ron Dennis eventually bought all of Teddy Mayer's shares in 1982, and assumed complete control of McLaren International. Dennis achieved his aim of making McLaren the leading F1 constructor when he won the title in 1984, with Niki Lauda driving and winning the F1 World Driver Championship. From then on, the team went from strength to strength. In 1985, 1988, 1989, 1990, and 1991, McLaren was F1 World Constructor Champion. In 1985, 1986, and 1989, Alain Prost won World Driver Championships driving McLaren cars; in 1988, 1990, and 1991, it was Ayrton Senna. In 1988, Prost and Senna won 15 of the 16 races run during the season!

During this winning period, the McLaren team cars used three different engines: from 1984 to 1987, the 1.5 TAG Porsche V-6 turbo; in 1988, the 1.5 Honda V-6 turbo; and, after F.I.A. changed the rules governing engines, when it was deemed that normal aspirated engines should be used, McLaren adopted the 3.5-liter Honda V-10. Since 1992, when Honda retired from GP racing, McLaren has used a variety of engines, from Ford to Peugeot. The present Mercedes-Benz engine has not been successful, as far as world championships go.

I have had the opportunity to witness and photograph the evolution of McLaren Cars, from their earliest days. The cars and drivers appearing in *McLaren Race Cars 1965 -1996 Photo Album* were photographed at venues throughout England. Included are an exciting variety of McLaren cars—true testimony to their success—which from their beginning in F1 Grand Prix racing in 1966 to the present day have won more than 100 Grand Prix races.

Norman Hayes
November 1996

Bruce McLaren in his own car, a MK 1A, at Oulton Park for the 1965 Tourist Trophy Race. McLaren ran the car with an automatic gearbox that gave him trouble throughout practice and also during the race, and eventually caused his retirement.

Frank Gardner driving a McLaren-Elva MK 1A with 4.7-liter Ford V-8, at Oulton Park for the 1966 R.A.C. Tourist Trophy. Gardner ran in second place for most of the race, but with only ten laps to go the engine broke a crankshaft.

Chris Amon in a MK 1A with 5.9-liter Chevrolet V-8, at a 1966 support race for the British Grand Prix. An accident on the first lap relegated Amon to the back of the field. With controlled aggression, he climbed back to finish in third place.

Bruce McLaren in a M4B with 2.2-liter B.R.M. engine, at the 1967 Race of Champions at Brands Hatch. McLaren missed a gear on the opening lap, the engine revs went sky high and the gearbox locked solid.

McLaren watched as his mechanics prepared his M4B for the 1967 International Spring Cup at Oulton Park.

McLaren entering the assembly area for the start of the 1967 International Spring Trophy Race at Oulton Park. McLaren finished in fifth place overall.

Alan Rollinson in the Formula 2 McLaren M4A with 1.6-liter Cosworth FVA engine. Rollinson finished tenth overall in the 1967 International Gold Cup race at Oulton Park.

Jo Bonnier driving the only 3-liter M5A B.R.M. V-12 car produced. Bonnier raced the car for the first time at the 1968 Race of Champions at Brands Hatch. He retired the car with steering and suspension problems.

McLaren at Druids Corner, Brands Hatch, during the 1968 Race of Champions. McLaren won the race in this M7A powered by a 3-liter Ford-Cosworth DFV V-8.

The winner of the 1968 Race of Champions, Bruce McLaren, and his McLaren M7A paraded round the track.

Mike Walker won the 1968 Guards Spring Cup Formula 3 race at Oulton Park in a McLaren M4A-Ford MAE.

Denny Hulme driving a M7A with 3-liter Ford DFV V-8, at the 1968 British Grand Prix at Brands Hatch. Hulme finished fourth despite gearbox problems.

Bruce McLaren in a M7A with 3-liter Ford DFV V-8, during the 1968 British Grand Prix. McLaren finished seventh overall.

The M7B, an experimental Formula 1 car built in 1969 for Bruce McLaren, with "pannier" fuel tanks and a 3-liter Ford Cosworth DFV V-8. The car did not finish in the Race of Champions at Brands Hatch due to an ignition problem.

The Guards 5000 Race, the first Formula 5000 race held in Great Britain, was run at Oulton Park in 1969. Peter Gethin in car no. 7, a McLaren M10A with 5.0-liter Bartz Chevrolet engine, led at Old Hall Corner.

Gethin drove a brilliant race to win the 1969 Guards 5000 Race by over a minute.

Derek Bell in the experimental 4WD M9A with 3-liter Ford-Cosworth DFV V-8, during the 1969 British Grand Prix at Silverstone. The car was retired in lap six with a broken rear suspension carrier.

Vic Elford in a M7B with 3-liter Ford-Cosworth DFV V-8, at the 1969 British Grand Prix. Elford finished in sixth place.

McLaren in command of his M7C with 3-liter Ford-Cosworth DFV V-8, specially built for his use. McLaren finished third overall in the 1969 British Grand Prix.

Start of the 1970 Race of Champions at Brands Hatch, with McLaren in car no. 4.

McLaren in his M14A with 3-liter Ford-Cosworth DFV V-8, at Druids Corner, Brands Hatch, during the 1970 Race of Champions.

McLaren crashed at Clearways and damaged the monocoque beyond repair.

Denny Hulme in car no. 5, a M14A with 3-liter Ford-Cosworth DFV V-8, finished third in the 1970 Race of Champions.

John Surtees in his M7C with 3-liter Ford-Cosworth DFV V-8, at the 1970 Race of Champions.

Mike Walker, winner of the 1970 Guards 5000 race at Oulton Park, in his Chevrolet-powered M10B.

Walker's M10B prior to the start of the
1970 Guards 5000 race.

Peter Gethin at Oulton Park during the 1970 Guards 5000 race. Gethin, driving a McLaren-Chevrolet M10B, finished second overall.

Howden Ganley driving a Chevrolet-powered M10B for the 1970 Guards 5000. Ganley finished third.

Hulme in a M14D with 3-liter Ford-Cosworth DFV V-8, during the 1970 British Grand Prix at Brands Hatch. Hulme, who had suffered badly burnt hands in an accident during practice for the Indianapolis 500, drove well and finished in third place overall.

Dan Gurney had a rather fruitless race at the 1970 British Grand Prix. He retired his M14A during the 61st lap with an overheated engine.

Gethin in his M14A with 3-liter Ford-Cosworth DFV V-8, during the 1971 Rothmans F1 International. Gethin, in the sole works car, finished the race in a close second.

Jody Scheckter, in his 2-liter Ford BDA-powered M21, moves through the paddock area prior to the 1972 John Players F2 Championship race at Mallory Park.

Scheckter in his M21 at Deers Leap, Oulton Park, during a heavy rain. Scheckter retired in lap 6 with no brakes in this 1972 John Players F2 Championship race.

Helmut Kelleners in a McLaren-Chevrolet M8F, at the 1972 Super Sports 200 Race at Silverstone. Kelleners had many problems during the race, but finished tenth overall.

Hans Wiedner in his McLaren-Chevrolet M8E, during the 1972 Super Sports 200 Race. Wiedner finished third overall.

Hulme, winner of the 1972 Rothmans International Gold Cup at Oulton Park, in his M19 with 3-liter Ford-Cosworth V-8. Hulme won by a large margin, setting a new circuit record of 117.76 mph.

Ray Calcutt driving a M18 with 5-liter Chevrolet V-8, during the 1972 Rothmans International Gold Cup race. Calcutt finished tenth overall.

Pierre Soukry drove a M10B with 5-liter Chevrolet V-8 to 11th place in the 1972 Rothmans International Gold Cup.

Peter Revson (no. 19) led the pack at Clearways during the 1972 British Grand Prix at Brands Hatch.

Revson took third in the 1972 British Grand Prix in his M19A powered by a 3-liter Ford-Cosworth V-8.

Hulme during the 1972 British Grand Prix. Hulme finished fifth in this M19A with 3-liter Ford-Cosworth DFV V-8.

The engine of Jody Scheckter's McLaren was changed prior to the 1972 World Championship Victory Race at Brands Hatch.

Tony Trimmer in his Chevrolet-powered M18 at the 1973 Rothmans 5000 European Championship. Trimmer finished seventh overall.

Trimmer passes Guy Edwards' Lola at Clay Hill during the 1973 Rothmans 5000 European Championship.

Hulme in his M23 with 3-liter Ford-Cosworth DFV V-8, at the 1973 Silverstone Formula 1 International Race. Hulme did not finish due to the engine's loss of oil pressure.

Hulme in his M23 for the 1974 BRDC Formula 1 International Trophy race at Silverstone.

Emerson Fittipaldi in his M23 with 3-liter Ford-Cosworth DFV V-8, for the 1975 Daily Express Trophy at Silverstone. Fittipaldi finished second.

J. Baker-Courtney in command of a McLaren-Elva with 4.7-liter Chevrolet V-8, at the 1975 Barbon Manor Hill Climb.

James Hunt, winner of the 1976 British Grand Prix at Brands Hatch, in his M23. Hunt and several others were involved in a collision at the start of the race. Hunt restarted and won the race handily. He was later disqualified on an appeal from Ferrari.

Jochen Mass in his M23-Ford DFV V-8. Mass burnt his clutch out on the starting line of the 1976 British Grand Prix.

Jochen Mass in his M26 powered by a 3-liter Ford DFV V-8, during the 1977 British Grand Prix at Silverstone. Mass finished fourth overall.

Brett Lunger in his M23-Ford DFV V-8, at the 1977 British Grand Prix. Lunger finished 13th.

Gilles Villeneuve, in a M23 with Ford DFV V-8, was an instant sensation in his first ever F1 race at the 1977 British Grand Prix. Villeneuve ran seventh, before having to pit for some minor problem, and went on to finish 11th.

D. C. Robinson in his McLaren sprint car at the 1977 Summer Sprint at Longridge.

James Hunt in his M26-Ford DFV V-8 during the 1978 British Grand Prix at Brands Hatch. Hunt spun and hit a barrier and did not finish.

Patrick Tambay, in his M26-Ford DFV V-8, finished the 1978 British Grand Prix in sixth place.

Wally Dallenbach during the 1978 Silverstone Indy Car Race. Dallenbach blew the engine of his McLaren M24B Indy car, and did not finish the race.

Salt Walther in his M24B-Ford-Cosworth 2.5-liter turbocharged DFX V-8 Indy car. Walther finished seventh in the 1978 Silverstone race.

Johnny Rutherford's M24B warming-up in the pits at the 1978 Silverstone Indy Car Race.

Rutherford on the track at Silverstone. He finished the race in fifth position.

Andrea de Cesaris in his McLaren MP4/1 with 3-liter Ford DFV V-8, at the 1981 British Grand Prix at Silverstone. He retired following an accident during the third lap.

John Watson, winner of the 1981 British Grand Prix, in his McLaren MP4/1.

Malcolm Clube in his 4.7-liter McLaren M1C, during a 1982 historic G.T. race at Brands Hatch.

David Franklin in his 5-liter McLaren M6B, during a 1982 historic G.T. race at Brands Hatch.

Niki Lauda's MP4B with 3-liter Ford DFV V-8, winner of the 1982 British Grand Prix.

70

Niki Lauda in his MP4/1C with 3-liter Ford DFV V-8, during the 1983 British Grand Prix. Lauda finished sixth.

John Watson in his MP4/1C-Ford DFV V-8 during the 1983 British Grand Prix.

Niki Lauda in his MP4/2 with TAG turbo 1.5 liter V-6, winner of the 1984 British Grand Prix at Brands Hatch.

A 1.5-liter TAG turbo V-6 engine in the McLaren pits at Silverstone for the 1985 British Grand Prix.

Alain Prost in his MP4/2B-TAG 1.5-liter turbo V-6 at the 1985 British Grand Prix.

Ray Bell driving a McLaren M8C-Chevrolet during a support race for the 1985 British Grand Prix.

John Foulston driving a McLaren-Chevrolet M8D during a support race for the 1985 British Grand Prix.

Prost, driving a McLaren MP4/2C-TAG Turbo V-6, finished third in the 1986 British Grand Prix at Brands Hatch.

Keke Rosberg's MP4/2C with 1.5-liter TAG turbo V-6, in the pits at the 1986 British Grand Prix at Brands Hatch.

Rosberg on the track at the 1986 British Grand Prix.

Stefan Johansson finished fourth in the 1987 British Grand Prix at Silverstone in this MP4/2C-TAG.

Prost finished second in the 1987 British Grand Prix in this MP4/3C with 1.5-liter TAG turbo V-6.

Ayrton Senna, driving a MP4/4 with 1.5-liter Honda Turbo, took the lead on lap 14 and held it through to the end of the 1988 British Grand Prix at Silverstone.

Senna, driving a MP4/4-Honda, spun off at Becketts on lap 12 and retired from the 1989 British Grand Prix.

At the 1989 British Grand Prix, Alain Prost won his 38th GP race in this MP4/5 with 1.5-liter Honda Turbo.

McLaren body shells on display in the pits during the 1990 British Grand Prix at Silverstone .

Gerhard Berger leaving the pits during the 1990 British Grand Prix at Silverstone. Berger, in second place in his McLaren-Honda MP4/5B, retired with only four laps to go—his throttle control mechanism failed.

Senna leaving the pits at the 1990 British Grand Prix. Senna finished third in his MP4/5B.

Berger at the 1991 British Grand Prix at Silverstone. Berger, in this McLaren-Honda MP4/6, finished the race in second position.

Senna during the 1991 British Grand Prix. Senna, in his 3.5-liter Honda-powered MP4/6, finished fourth after he ran out of fuel and dropped from first during the last lap.

At the 1992 British GP at Silverstone, Senna, in his McLaren-Honda MP4/7, did not finish due to a broken gearbox.

Berger, in his MP4/7, finished the 1992 British Grand Prix in fifth position—his engine exploding as he crossed the finishing line!

Ayrton Senna's McLaren MP4/8 with Ford HB V-8, in the pits at the 1993 British Grand Prix at Silverstone.

David Coulthard, in his McLaren MP4/11 with 3-liter Mercedes V-10, moved up from tenth place after a bad start to finish a creditable fifth overall in the 1996 British Grand Prix.

Mika Hakkinen, in his McLaren MP4/11, finished third at the 1996 British Grand Prix.

McLaren Cars' success has been, in no small part, due to the caliber of drivers associated with the marque. In the remaining pages, we salute some of the best.

Howden Ganley in the paddock at Oulton Park for the 1970 Guards 5000 Car Race.

Dan Gurney on the parade lap for the 1970 British Grand Prix at Brands Hatch.

Jody Sheckter in his McLaren M21 in the assembly area at Oulton Park, 1972.

Peter Revson in the pit area prior to the 1973 Formula 1 International Race at Silverstone.

Emerson Fittipaldi on the winner's float following the 1975 John Player Grand Prix at Silverstone.

100

Denny Hulme (right).

John Surtees.

Frank Gardner.

Derek Bell.

Peter Gethin.

James Hunt.

Jochen Mass.

Niki Lauda.

Ayrton Senna.

The Iconografix Photo Archive Series includes:

AMERICAN CULTURE

AMERICAN SERVICE STATIONS 1935-1943	ISBN 1-882256-27-1
COCA-COLA: A HISTORY IN PHOTOGRAPHS 1930-1969	ISBN 1-882256-46-8
COCA-COLA: ITS VEHICLES IN PHOTOGRAPHS 1930-1969	ISBN 1-882256-47-6
PHILLIPS 66 1945-1954	ISBN 1-882256-42-5

AUTOMOTIVE

FERRARI PININFARINA 1952-1996	ISBN 1-882256-65-4
GT40	ISBN 1-882256-64-6
IMPERIAL 1955-1963	ISBN 1-882256-22-0
IMPERIAL 1964-1968	ISBN 1-882256-23-9
LE MANS 1950: THE BRIGGS CUNNINGHAM CAMPAIGN	ISBN 1-882256-21-2
LINCOLN MOTOR CARS 1920-1942	ISBN 1-882256-57-3
LINCOLN MOTOR CARS 1946-1960	ISBN 1-882256-58-1
MG 1945-1964	ISBN 1-882256-52-2
MG 1965-1980	ISBN 1-882256-53-0
PACKARD MOTOR CARS 1935-1942	ISBN 1-882256-44-1
PACKARD MOTOR CARS 1946-1958	ISBN 1-882256-45-X
SEBRING 12-HOUR RACE 1970	ISBN 1-882256-20-4
STUDEBAKER 1933-1942	ISBN 1-882256-24-7
STUDEBAKER 1946-1958	ISBN 1-882256-25-5
VANDERBILT CUP RACE 1936 & 1937	ISBN 1-882256-66-2

TRACTORS AND CONSTRUCTION EQUIPMENT

CASE TRACTORS 1912-1959	ISBN 1-882256-32-8
CATERPILLAR MILITARY TRACTORS VOLUME 1	ISBN 1-882256-16-6
CATERPILLAR MILITARY TRACTORS VOLUME 2	ISBN 1-882256-17-4
CATERPILLAR SIXTY	ISBN 1-882256-05-0
CLETRAC AND OLIVER CRAWLERS	ISBN 1-882256-43-3
ERIE SHOVEL	ISBN 1-882256-69-7
FARMALL CUB	ISBN 1-882256-71-9
FARMALL F–SERIES	ISBN 1-882256-02-6
FARMALL MODEL H	ISBN 1-882256-03-4
FARMALL MODEL M	ISBN 1-882256-15-8
FARMALL REGULAR	ISBN 1-882256-14-X
FARMALL SUPER SERIES	ISBN 1-882256-49-2
FORDSON 1917-1928	ISBN 1-882256-33-6
HART-PARR	ISBN 1-882256-08-5
HOLT TRACTORS	ISBN 1-882256-10-7
INTERNATIONAL TRACTRACTOR	ISBN 1-882256-48-4
INTERNATIONAL TD CRAWLERS 1933-1962	ISBN 1-882256-72-7
JOHN DEERE MODEL A	ISBN 1-882256-12-3
JOHN DEERE MODEL B	ISBN 1-882256-01-8

JOHN DEERE MODEL D	ISBN 1-882256-00-X
JOHN DEERE 30 SERIES	ISBN 1-882256-13-1
MINNEAPOLIS-MOLINE U-SERIES	ISBN 1-882256-07-7
OLIVER TRACTORS	ISBN 1-882256-09-3
RUSSELL GRADERS	ISBN 1-882256-11-5
TWIN CITY TRACTOR	ISBN 1-882256-06-9

RAILWAYS

CHICAGO, ST. PAUL, MINNEAPOLIS & OMAHA RAILWAY 1880-1940	ISBN 1-882256-67-0
CHICAGO&NORTH WESTERN RAILWAY 1975-1995	ISBN 1-882256-76-X
GREAT NORTHERN RAILWAY 1945-1970	ISBN 1-882256-56-5
MILWAUKEE ROAD 1850-1960	ISBN 1-882256-61-1
SOO LINE 1975-1992	ISBN 1-882256-68-9
WISCONSIN CENTRAL LIMITED 1987-1996	ISBN 1-882256-75-1

TRUCKS

BEVERAGE TRUCKS 1910-1975	ISBN 1-882256-60-3
BROCKWAY TRUCKS 1948-1961*	ISBN 1-882256-55-7
DODGE TRUCKS 1929-1947	ISBN 1-882256-36-0
DODGE TRUCKS 1948-1960	ISBN 1-882256-37-9
LOGGING TRUCKS 1915-1970	ISBN 1-882256-59-X
MACK® MODEL AB*	ISBN 1-882256-18-2
MACK AP SUPER-DUTY TRUCKS 1926-1938*	ISBN 1-882256-54-9
MACK MODEL B 1953-1966 VOLUME 1*	ISBN 1-882256-19-0
MACK MODEL B 1953-1966 VOLUME 2*	ISBN 1-882256-34-4
MACK EB-EC-ED-EE-EF-EG-DE 1936-1951*	ISBN 1-882256-29-8
MACK EH-EJ-EM-EQ-ER-ES 1936-1950*	ISBN 1-882256-39-5
MACK FC-FCSW-NW 1936-1947*	ISBN 1-882256-28-X
MACK FG-FH-FJ-FK-FN-FP-FT-FW 1937-1950*	ISBN 1-882256-35-2
MACK LF-LH-LJ-LM-LT 1940-1956 *	ISBN 1-882256-38-7
MACK MODEL B FIRE TRUCKS 1954-1966*	ISBN 1-882256-62-X
MACK MODEL CF FIRE TRUCKS 1967-1981*	ISBN 1-882256-63-8
STUDEBAKER TRUCKS 1927-1940	ISBN 1-882256-40-9
STUDEBAKER TRUCKS 1941-1964	ISBN 1-882256-41-7

* This product is sold under license from Mack Trucks, Inc. All rights reserved.

The Iconografix Photo Album Series includes:

CORVETTE PROTOTYPES & SHOW CARS	ISBN 1-882256-77-8
LOLA RACE CARS 1962-1990	ISBN 1-882256-73-5
McLAREN RACE CARS 1965-1996	ISBN 1-882256-74-3

The Iconografix Photo Gallery Series includes:

CATERPILLAR PHOTO GALLERY	ISBN 1-882256-70-0

All Iconografix books are available from direct mail specialty book dealers and bookstores worldwide, or can be ordered from the publisher. For book trade and distribution information or to add your name to our mailing list contact

Iconografix
PO Box 446
Hudson, Wisconsin, 54016

Telephone: (715) 381-9755
(800) 289-3504 (USA)
Fax: (715) 381-9756

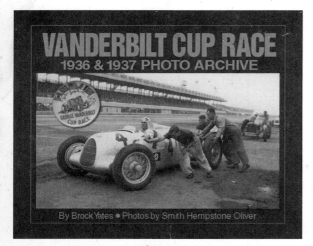

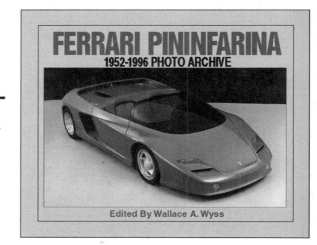

MORE
GREAT BOOKS FROM
ICONOGRAFIX

VANDERBILT CUP RACE 1936 & 1937
Photo Archive ISBN 1-882256-66-2

FERRARI PININFARINA 1952-1996
Photo Archive ISBN 1-88225665-4

GT40 *Photo Archive*
ISBN 1-882256-64-6

LOLA RACE CARS 1962-1990
Photo Album ISBN 1-882256-73-5

**LEMANS 1950: THE BRIGGS
CUNNINGHAM CAMPAIGN**
Photo Archive ISBN 1-882256-21-2

**CORVETTE PROTOTYPES &
SHOW CARS** *Photo Album*
ISBN 1-882256-77-8

SEBRING 12-HOUR RACE 1970
Photo Arhive ISBN 1-882256-20-4

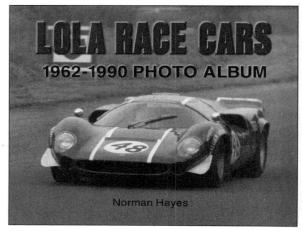

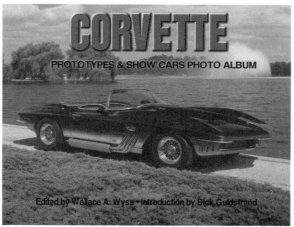